Paid To Talk:
A Journey Into Voice Acting

By Michael Lenz

Acknowledgments:

I want to thank Emma, Jake, Natey, and Gabriel, for putting up with having to be super quiet while Daddy is recording. I also want to thank my friend, editor, and business partner, Jason Noxon, for his technical and creative support. And of course, thanks most of all to my beautiful wife Dianna, for being my best friend, my greatest encouragement, and the love of my life.

Introduction:

Have you ever wondered what it would be like to be a professional voice actor, but didn't have a clue how to start? Author and professional voice actor Michael Lenz wondered the same thing when he began his journey into the world of voice acting.

Join Michael as he shares with you the valuable lessons he learned as he worked his way from the ground up to fulfill his dream of becoming a professional voice actor and audio book narrator.

Paid To Talk - A Journey Into Voice Acting is essential reading for anyone interested in learning about what it takes to make it in this competitive industry. In addition to the insight he gained from industry insiders, Michael also shares interesting first hand accounts of his journey from a complete novice to becoming a narrator for one of the leading audio book publishing companies in the world.

Filled with great insights and helpful advice, Paid To Talk - A Journey Into Voice Acting is certain to inspire and guide you as you begin your own journey into the amazing profession of voice acting!

Table of Contents:

Chapter 1:

My Story – Why I Wrote This Book

"So...what do you do?"

We've all been asked this question many times, haven't we?

Many of us are fortunate to be able to answer proudly, knowing that we're doing exactly what we were meant to do in this life. Some of us, however, answer the question truthfully, but in the back of our minds we wish we were saying something else.

If you've been asked that question, and you wish you could answer "I'm a professional voice actor," but you truthfully had to give a different answer, then my hope is that this book will help you gain the knowledge and confidence to take the steps necessary to make your dream a reality.

This book is about my journey.

Let me start by telling you what I'm not. I'm not a professionally trained stage or film actor. I'm not a well-connected industry insider with tips on how to beat the system. I'm not a voice-over trainer trying to drum up business.

I'm just like you.

I'm someone who had an interest in voice acting and started out by learning as much as I could about the industry. Along the way, I've made some mistakes but also achieved some level of success. Early on, I found it difficult to gain information about this pretty competitive industry, but with persistence I was able to carve out a professional voice over career that is continuing to evolve every day.

I decided to start a blog several years ago so that I could share my journey with fellow voice actors in hopes of helping others learn and to learn from others. After three years of compiling posts, I decided to create a book to take all this information and provide it in one, concise format.

'Paid To Talk – A Journey Into Voice Acting' is the result.

So I thought I'd explain the start of my journey by answering the way I would if I was asked the question "So...what do you do?"

First let me tell you that I don't do voice acting full time. I'm a partner in a successful small business that occupies much of my time. I really like being a small-business owner, but I've never been one of those people who can only do one thing to the exclusion of everything else. I have to do other things - I like diversity, and I love to create.

One of the "other things" I used to do was serve in public office. I was on the City Council in my hometown and served as Mayor for one term. After eight years of service, my time in public office came to an end (that's a fancy way of saying I lost an election) and after leaving public office my life took a completely different turn.

I suddenly had a lot of free time to spend exploring other interests in my life.

I knew that I had enjoyed communicating when in public office (making speeches, talking on the radio and television and the like) and I also had an unexplored interest in screenwriting. That interest led me to a local filmmakers group where, at one of the meetings, a marketing representative for a local voice training company handed out post cards outlining their business.

I was blown away by the possibility of getting paid to talk.

I had some idea about what voice acting was, but had never seriously looked into it. Suddenly it dawned on me that I could continue to do what I'd most enjoyed about politics, to use my voice to communicate, but I didn't have to get elected to do it!

I was hooked.

I knew I wanted to find out more about this exciting industry, but had no idea where to start. Even though I was a bit wary, I figured I'd go talk with the company that offered training, at least to get more information, so I made an appointment to meet with them.

Little did I know that doing so would change the path of my life forever.

Chapter 2:

To Train or Not To Train

Finally, the day of my appointment with the voice coaching company came and the initial meeting was incredibly informative. The owner shocked me by telling me that 75% of all voice actors who get trained rarely find work.

That didn't sound like a great way to promote his business; however, he went on to tell me that if you can manage to be in the other 25%, you've already eliminated most of the competition. After about an hour meeting, I was convinced that voice acting was something I wanted to do, and I set my goal to be in that 25% category.

I made the decision to invest a pretty hefty sum of money into getting trained, and looking back, I can say that it was the best decision I made to start my career - which brings me to some important words of wisdom:

Words of Wisdom: *Get trained - especially if you have no previous acting experience. The most important step you can take is to get trained by a reputable voice training company. Getting paid to talk may sound easy, but it's actually very competitive, and producers can spot an amateur from a mile away.*

There are very basic things you'll learn in training that will separate you from those who aren't prepared.

I was told by one producer about a man he had met at a party who was not a professional voice actor, but had what the producer believed was the perfect voice for a project. He brought the man in for a read and....he was awful. He had a wonderful tone to his voice in conversation, but hand him a piece of paper with copy on it and his tone and pacing changed completely. He was stiff and sounded, well, like he was reading off a piece of paper. So,guess who got the job instead... you guessed it - me.

The producer called me in for a read and asked if I could voice the part in a particular tone and pacing that was different than my usual voice. Being a professionally trained voice actor, I voiced the copy as directed and he was very happy. After the session, he recounted the story to me, and told me he would never again use anyone other than a professional for voice jobs.

Back to my training. Everything I thought I knew about voice acting was thrown out the window after my first training session. The ability to read and interpret copy may come easily to some people, but for most of us, this is a learned art form.

Remember, voice acting is acting with your voice...and *only* your voice.

Other forms of acting that involve the visual realm allow the actor to convey emotions and feelings through body and facial movements and expressions.

You could argue that those actors have a distinct advantage in being able convey their meaning. Voice actors are never seen, only heard and yet we still need to convey a full range of emotions and feelings with only our voice.

During my initial training, my eyes were truly opened to the importance – and difficulty – of making the listener believe what you are saying, and not ever think you are simply reading words on a piece of paper. Easier said than done!

After listening to my initial practice read, I realized how bad I sounded. The good news is that after some direction from my teacher I did another recording, incorporating all of his pointers. Listening to the second recording, I was amazed at the improvement. I was convinced, and to this day I am a firm believer, that voice actors should never stop training.

Think about it, even the best athletes in the world constantly train. Think about Peyton Manning or Michael Jordan – both, even in their prime, practiced all the time to maintain their competitive edge.

It does cost money to get trained, but it's worth the investment. If you'd like more info on the company I used, you can contact me through my website, mikelenzvoice.com, and I'll get you in touch with them.

Chapter 3:

So You Got Trained – Now What?

So let's say you invest in training and learn all about becoming a professional voice actor...now what?

That's the beginning of perhaps the most difficult part of the journey.

The next step is to create your demo. This is your calling card, the one thing in many cases, which will make or break your chances of voice-over success. So make sure it's done well!

The company that I trained with provided demo development and production as part of the training package and, in my estimation, any reputable voice training company should provide the same service.

So, my training was over and I was fired up and ready to go, but I had to wait...and wait...and wait for my demo to be mixed and mastered. Now, it only took about three weeks, mind you, but it seemed like an eternity.

Once my demo arrived, the next step was to get CD cases and a kick butt cover. Well actually, the next step was to invite my whole family over to listen to my demo. My heart was pounding as I placed the CD in the stereo and pushed "Play." I knew I'd done something right when my mother asked "who's that?" after the CD was done playing.

Anyway, back to our story...CD case and cover...oh yeah, here come some more words of wisdom.

> ***Words of Wisdom:*** *There are very basic things that need to be on the spine of your CD cover - like your name and contact info. Sounds simple, but I've been told that some*

actors forget to do this. It's important to put your information on the spine because CD's are usually stacked with the spine pointed out. A producer can quickly scan the stack and see which talent he or she wants at a glance.

Also, don't put your face on your CD cover - remember you're a VOICE actor. I was told by one of the top voice talent agents in the country that he hates to know what a voice talent looks like. He wants it to be all about the voice, and if you think about it, he's right.

You've been trained to act with your voice, not your face.

So back to my journey... To save money, I was able to work with a friend who's a graphic artist and web designer who was branching out into audio and video production. I made a deal with him to trade some future voice work for a CD cover and business card design, logo, and letterhead. That's about all you really need to get started promoting yourself. I was pretty psyched when my CD cover was done, and the best part was that I had secured a future voice acting job in the process!

At this point I had gone through three months of voice training, gotten my demo produced, and now had a CD cover, a cool logo, business cards, and some letterhead. Now all I had to do was go get a job. Easy enough...or so I thought.

Chapter 4:

Persistence

Getting through all of the preparation for launching your voice-over career can be a long process. After all, as we've talked about, you go through all the training, wait for your demo to be made, create a logo, CD cover, business cards, letterhead and maybe even a website. It all takes time, but the fun thing about it is that it's all really tangible stuff. I remember when I finally had my finished demo and cover in my hand. It was extremely satisfying.

The next step is taking the plunge to go out and market yourself and land that first job.

Now, you may be one of the lucky few who get a job right way. If so, congratulations! If you're like the rest of us though, it will take time - sometimes a long time. This is a critical point in your journey, so here are some more hopefully insightful words of wisdom:

> **Words of Wisdom:** Don't get discouraged if you don't get a paid voice-over job right away. The average time it takes to get your first job is about seven months. That is almost exactly the amount of time it took me. But here's the thing - the majority of people who get trained to be voice actors give up within the first year. In fact, my teacher told me the number is around 75%! That means if you just hang in there for a year, you'll be way ahead of most of your competition.

So what do you do to promote yourself? There are many ways to market your services. I'll share with you a couple of things I did to keep myself fresh and to continue to develop contacts in the industry:

1. **I found all the production companies in my area that might need voice actors.** Ask your friends if they know of anyone who might need your services. You'll be amazed who might know someone or some company. Your friends will think it's really neat that you are a voice actor. After all, it's not very common and let's face it - it is pretty cool! Check the yellow pages, read the local business journals, talk to your local chamber of commerce. I did all of these things and created a list of companies. I then called and introduced myself, told them I was a voice actor, and asked if I could send them my demo. The goal should be to get rid of all of your demos as quickly as possible. And about a week after you send out your demo, give the company another call to make sure they received it.

2. **I gave my business cards out to everyone I saw.** This was in fact the way I got my very first paid job. I attended a luncheon one day and a man walked up and introduced himself. He was the person who had produced the media for my first Mayoral race. I had never met him before, but he knew who I was. He handed me his card, and I took the opportunity to tell him about my new voice-over career. I gave him my card and told him to please call if he ever needed my help. As it turned out he called me several weeks later and asked if I could do a "hard read." Not knowing what a "hard read" meant, I immediately answered "of course!" A week later I was in a studio recording a radio ad for a local car dealership. So you never know what will come of giving someone your business card. Give them out all day long!

3. **Play to your strengths.** I love to talk to people about what they do. The truth is, everyone has an interesting story to tell, and we all like to talk

about ourselves don't we? When I talk to other part time voice actors, one of my first questions is "what do you do when you're not voice acting?" The answer to this question may be the key to your voice-over niche.

What do I mean by playing to your strengths? Well, I'll use myself as an example, because as I just wrote, we all like to talk about ourselves, right? . Being in the medical field, I deal with drug names and medical terminology all day long. When you start to think about it, there are many applications for this type of background in the voice-over world.

In order to distinguish myself, I always include this information in all of my correspondence with producers, and it has led to a number of jobs. For example: I was hired by a publishing company to voice 300 generic and brand name drugs for an audio glossary in a nursing handbook that they were producing. I also voiced the part of a Doctor doing dictation for the CD insert in a textbook on Medical Transcription.

In both cases, I was hired specifically because I have knowledge of medical terminology. These jobs have led to even more work with this company because once I did the first job, and did it very professionally (because I was trained), they knew I was reliable.

I was also able to become an audio book narrator as a direct result of my medical background. The first book I narrated had a great deal of medical terminology, and the publisher told me that she chose me not only because she liked my audition, but also because she felt I would be familiar with the terms. By making sure my background in the medical field was part of my bio information, I was able to land my first audio book!

Take a little time and think about what it is that you do in your current job, and what applications there may be for your skills in the voice-over world. A voice actor I know is a former State Trooper. He used his experience in the law enforcement field to pitch a training module concept to his State organization. They thought it was a great idea and funded the project. He is in charge of the project and does all the voice-over work on the modules.

Whatever your particular knowledge base is, use it to set yourself apart from the competition, and create a marketing niche for yourself. This is a great way to land that first job.

I truly believe that if you take these steps and be persistent (remember you want to be in that 25% category) you will land that first job.

In the next chapter we'll talk about how important that first job is and what you need to do to leave a great impression, and get more work in the process.

Chapter 5:

You Got Your First Gig!
(Or Maybe Not)

As I mentioned in the previous chapter, it may take some time to get your first paid gig, or you may be fortunate to get work fairly quickly after completing your training. In this chapter we'll discuss what to do when your first job comes along...and what to do if it doesn't.

So let's say you just landed your first voice-over job. Now all you have to do is show up to the studio and deliver the perfect read. No pressure. I mean, really, how hard could it be?

No matter how well you were trained, no matter how much you've practiced the script, your first job will probably be nerve-wracking. There are a few things that will help you though:

1. **It's OK to be a little nervous.** Even star athletes at the top of their game – the aforementioned Peyton Manning, and Michael Jordan for example – admit to being nervous before they're about to perform. Great stage actors admit to being nervous before the big show. Being nervous is normal. What professionally trained athletes, and actors have in common, though, is that when the time comes to perform, they kick into gear and do what has come to be natural for them, due to their training. The same is true for you.

2. **Listen to your producer.** You are being paid to voice the copy the way the client and producer direct you to. Your specific job is to listen to their direction and give them what they want. Don't offer your opinion unless asked. My trainer and several

producers I've worked with have told me that the most important quality they look for in a voice actor is his or her ability to take direction.

3.   **Be prepared.** It sounds almost too simple to mention, but it's important to have read the copy (if possible) before you do your read. Most producers will provide you with the copy prior to the recording session. But don't be surprised if many changes are made on the fly while you're in the booth. That's why part of being prepared means bringing a pencil...that's right, you will need to mark up the copy as direction comes flying at you. If you try to do it from memory, you're asking for trouble. Being professional means coming prepared - a pencil and water are essential in the recording booth.

4.   **Don't get discouraged.** Many times you will go into the recording booth and give a read that you think is pretty darn good, only to be bombarded with changes from the producer's booth. As you go through

take after take, your confidence level begins to drop. I can tell you from personal experience that many of my best reads came on the take after I had just about completely given up on myself. A producer that I frequently work with gave me advice early on: he told me that he knows what read he wants, he can hear it in his head. He just doesn't have the ability to read it. That's why he hires voice talent. "Never take direction personally", he told me. Even the best voice-actors get worked over by producers. Our job is to stay focused and concentrate on delivering what the producer wants.

If you can embrace your nervousness, know that you are prepared, take direction well, and not get discouraged in the booth, you'll come out of your first voice-over job in great shape...and you'll have started a positive relationship with a producer that will hopefully lead to more work.

Getting your first voice-over job is pretty exciting, and something to be proud of. It's a good feeling to have your hard work and financial investment pay off. If you haven't gotten a job yet, please don't get discouraged. Like anything in life worth achieving, you have to be willing to hang in there until you meet up with success.

Oprah Winfrey once said, **"Luck is preparation meeting opportunity."** I strongly believe that. You can be prepared and never get an opportunity (bummer), and you can get an opportunity and not be prepared for it (real bummer). But when you work hard and prepare yourself *and* that opportunity comes along, then you're ready to take advantage of that "luck" that came your way.

As I said in an earlier post, my first professional voice-over job was the result of **"luck."** When I met the producer who had handled the media for my first Mayoral campaign, I was in a position to hand him by new business card and ask him to keep me in mind for future work. If I hadn't done the **"preparation"** part by getting trained, creating my demo, and printing business cards, I wouldn't have been in a position to take advantage of the **"opportunity"** presented to me by talking with a person who hired voice-over artists. In this case, preparation met opportunity and I received a call a few weeks later from this producer, asking me to do the voice-over for a local car commercial.

In the meantime, there are other things you can do to network and hone your skills while working toward your first job. Here are some more words of wisdom:

> **Words of Wisdom:** *Stay busy, even if it means volunteering your voice. Now I know there are some voice-over artists who don't agree with me. Your voice is valuable, and you shouldn't lessen its value by doing anything for free, they say. I respectfully disagree. Early in your voice-over career, you need to get your name out into the community, and a great way to do that, and to help out a good cause, is to volunteer.*
>
> *One of the things I did was to contact my local PBS station and volunteer for a wonderful program they offered for the blind and print disabled. Volunteers go into a recording studio and read local*

newspapers and magazines live over the air. It's a great way to practice, and to participate in a very worthwhile program.

Another thing I did was join a local film makers group. If there's one in your area, this is a great way to meet other artists and to make connections that could help in the future. I met a man who was producing a stellar documentary that will soon be seen across the country. He and his partners were still in the filming stages and looking for further funding. I helped out with some fund raising and volunteered my services to voice a short trailer they were using to promote the documentary (I even got a small on camera role!)

One more example - a fellow voice over artist I know started a volunteer program in which voice actors go into hospitals and read stories to children. What a fantastic way to give back to your community and increase your network of friends in the voice-over business.

So remember - stay busy, volunteer, expand your network, and always be prepared for that opportunity that's just around the corner.

Chapter 6:

Building Relationships

This may not be so amazing to many of you out there, but one of the best ways to build relationships in the voice over industry is through social networking.

For those of you who haven't yet discovered social networking, check out sites like Facebook and Twitter. At these sites you can create a personal profile and post information about yourself. It's a great way to stay in touch with friends you might not otherwise communicate with. It's also a fantastic way to let your network of friends know what you're up to.

After I finished building my home recording studio (more on this in Chapter 9) , I posted a comment on Facebook.

I happened to get a friend request from someone who I hadn't seen in a while. I accepted her request and she was then able to go to my account and see what I was up to. That day she sent me a message telling me that she had checked out my website (which was posted on my account) and said she might like to use my services for some ads she was going to be producing soon. Just one post had led to potential future work. Pretty amazing!

And the best thing about social networking is that it's free. When your starting out in the voice acting business, free is a good thing. Guerrilla marketing, and thinking outside of the box are essential to getting the word out about the services you provide.

Words of Wisdom: *Make sure that you engage visitors to your social network site on a personal level. I recently read an analysis of social media sites by Larry Frieders. He determined that the key to success is* *engagement and communication on a personal level. Every word and shared experience is part of the overall marketing mixture. Larry says, "people who decide to engage their "tribe" must do so honestly, openly, and in the guise of a real person, a real friend."*

I've really enjoyed using these social networking sites to stay in touch with old friends and make a bunch of new friends who are passionate about the things that I'm passionate about. Within each social media site (Facebook, Twitter, LinkedIn, etc.) you can find forums and groups specific to your particular interests. Search for voice actor groups and you'll be amazed at how many "friends" you'll find who are on the same journey as you. These groups are a tremendous source of information and inspiration. The world is truly getting smaller and smaller, and we all have so much to share.

Try to dedicate at least a half-hour each day to social networking. This isn't new to many of you, but for me it's been pretty amazing. I've been on Facebook and Twitter for a while, but recently I've been paying close attention to my posts and tweets and to the responses I get.

These responses have led me to some great sites and suggestions. We all tend to spend most of our time telling everyone about ourselves. By spending more time following and listening, I've learned some great stuff. In the voice-over business, there are so many ways to find leads and jobs.

The more we all listen, the more we'll all get to talk. So take some time each day to pay attention to your social networking and let the path it takes you on lead you to some interesting places - - and more work!

Now that I've extolled the virtues of social networking, allow me to add one caveat. Social networking is great. It's a useful tool for getting yourself noticed. Nothing, however, can replace the energy that occurs when you talk with a real live person face to face and share ideas and your passion for the world of voice-overs.

An example of this can be best illustrated by my entry into the world of audiobook narration, which was a result of just such a personal conversation with a fellow voice actor.

An individual named Jason who was just getting started in the voice over world contacted me. He asked if we could grab some breakfast and talk about my perspective on what it takes to make it in the voice over industry.

We had a great talk, and he shared with me his background in the field of audio engineering (an area that is definitely not my strong point). Jason mentioned a site that he had found that accepted auditions for audiobook narrations. I checked out the site and decided to send in some auditions.

Several weeks later, I was contacted by a publisher who had selected me as the narrator for an award-winning book. I was thrilled to have the opportunity, but was also a bit concerned that I would be responsible for the complete production of the audiobook.

As it turned out, I reached out to Jason and asked if he wanted to be the editor on the project. He agreed, and what began as a simple breakfast, turned into a business venture and ultimately to a great friendship. We're now in the process of creating our own production company and collaborate on fun projects all the time.

So make sure you not only focus on your social networking, but also be sure to get out from behind your computer and actually talk with someone! It's invigorating and fun, and I guarantee you'll learn something you hadn't thought of. You'll also be nurturing or beginning a friendship - and that can never be a bad thing.

Chapter 7:

Never Stop Learning

The fact that you're reading this book is proof that you are committed to learning all you can about the voice over industry. You should be very proud of yourself, because too many people seem to think that they don't need to constantly strive to learn. Too many potential voice actors think that they don't need to be trained, or don't need to constantly work to hone their talent.

To be honest with you, when I first heard about voice acting, I was one of those people. After all, I had been Mayor of my hometown. I was very skilled at speaking to groups, speaking on television and the radio. I read out loud to my wife and children. How hard could it be? The simple truth is that it's very hard. But, like most things that are difficult to attain, it is worth the time, effort and investment.

We've covered this in previous chapters, but it is worth repeating. When you look at the greatest athletes today, or throughout history for that matter, you will find one thing that they all have in common: they never stop learning. The greatest athletes spend much more time practicing then they do performing.

Another great example are those in the music industry. Think about your favorite musical artist and how much time they have to invest in their craft.. I was at a concert recently listening to my favorite band, and I was blown away by how incredible they sounded - not only individually - but also how they blended together perfectly to create an amazing performance.

As I sat watching and listening, it dawned on me that each of the musicians in the band must have spent countless hours practicing to become an accomplished musician in their own right. On top of all the time they spent alone, add all the hours of time spent working with the other members of the band to create a seamless performance. What I was fortunate enough to watch in two hours, they had spent years of their lives perfecting.

No matter where you are in your voice acting career, you always have room to grow and improve. If you're just beginning your journey and feel overwhelmed, I know how you feel because I was there not long ago! Believe me when I tell you that if you are willing to learn and seek out the knowledge, you will succeed, and there are a lot of fellow voice actors who are willing to help.

If you have specific questions, you can always drop me a line at mikelenzvoice.com. I will respond and if I don't know the answer, I'll direct you to someone or somewhere for help in finding the answer.

One of my favorite quotes is "The longest journey begins with one step".... I love that line. In life we so often envision our dreams and immediately believe we'll attain them overnight. We see others living the "perfect" life, and imagine ourselves doing the same thing. I bet if you looked below the surface of any person you believe has reached a level of success that you aspire to, you'd find out that he or she has been working hard to achieve that "overnight" success for a long, long time.

If voice acting is your passion, keep working at it every day and watch how you progress. Try this test: Every morning when you wake up, commit to doing three things that will move you along in your journey. Write them down - - and then do them. Do this for one month, keeping track of each day's goals and accomplishments. After the month, take a look at where you are and where you began. My bet is you'll have progressed much further than you thought.

Keep your mind open to the possibilities in front of you. As I mentioned earlier, a simple email from a fellow voice actor led to a friendship, a professional collaboration and the beginnings of a production company. Every connection is important!

Chapter 8:

Finding Your Niche

The world of voice acting is very broad and diverse, and it's easy to get lost in all the information out there. Information overload can sometimes result in action paralysis. When I first started out, I was eager to find out as much as I could about this exciting industry. The more I found out, the more excited I got...and the more confused about what direction to focus on.

As I mentioned earlier, my background is in the medical profession, and I also had political experience, having served as Finance Commissioner as well as Mayor of my hometown. I figured these should be part of any cover letter I sent and any conversation I had with prospective producers, or with anyone I talked to about my voice over career, for that matter. I thought of them as my calling card – things about me that would distinguish me from everyone else.

It worked.

At the beginning of my marketing efforts - after completing my demos and cover letters – I called every production company and radio station in the area where I lived. I sent follow up letters, and made follow-up phone calls. In each instance I would mention my background in the medical profession and that I had served as Mayor.

At one point I was searching the Internet looking to see if there were any talent agencies in the area that might be able to represent me. I came across one company and gave them a call. A woman answered the phone and we began a conversation. As I went through my pitch, I mentioned the medical background and Mayor things. She stopped me and said she knew me. As it turns out, she was the creative director for one of the largest production companies in my area. This company had a sister company talent agency – the very one that I had found while searching the Internet!

She told me she remembered talking with me the week before. "You're the guy who was Mayor," she said.

Bingo!

We had a nice conversation, and she gave me some good advice about my demo. I went out and did exactly what she told me to do and about a month later I sent her my reworked demo. Two weeks later I received an email from her casting me in a radio commercial for a regional insurance company.

Words of Wisdom: Figure out what distinguishes you from the competition and make that a constant part of your marketing plan. You are unique, with particular areas of your background that could determine your niche within the voice over industry. Remember the retired state trooper I told you about? After he retired, he trained to become a voice actor. He then approached the State Troopers Association and convinced them to hire him to take all of their manuals and make them available in audio form. Of course he did all the voice over work on the project!

Early in my voice over career, I was chosen for a number of medical related projects, specifically because of my medical background, and familiarity with hard to pronounce medical terminology. The producers knew this about me, because I made sure to tell them.

No matter what your background, you can be creative and memorable by incorporating what makes you unique into every pitch you make for a potential voice over gig. Remember, this is a very competitive industry, and producers get inundated with demos all the time. You need to do all you can to set yourself apart from the crowd, and when determining what niche you want to focus on, look at your background, your interests, and you expertise. Then do your research to determine if there is a specific area within the voice over industry that would benefit from your specific abilities. It's a great way to focus your efforts and break into the voice over world. Where it takes you after that, you never know!

Chapter 9:

Home Recording Studio

So, at the beginning of my journey into the world of voice acting I took several important steps:

1. Completed my training with one of the top voice-over training companies in the country.

2. Created my demo CD, with both commercial and narrative samples.

3. Created business cards and letterhead

4. Sent out letters and demos to all of the local producers and radio stations.

5. Started booking local and regional voice-over jobs.

6. Accumulated some money from the work I'd done..

The logical next step was to create a small home recording studio. Why, you might ask, would I do that? Well, the reason is that having the ability to record in your own studio opens up an entire other realm of possible voice-over work.

In today's fast-paced world, companies are looking to turn their projects around very quickly. In many cases, companies need the voice-over portion of the project done within a 24 to 48 hour time frame. Finding a producer, and a studio to record in, and scheduling time to have the voice talent come in and record can be very time consuming. This process also limits a company to only utilizing talent that is within a certain geographic proximity.

With the Internet, companies can now go out and seek talent from anywhere in the world, and that is exactly what they do. These companies have tapped into the power of the Internet to bring producers and casting agents seeking voice talent together with voice actors seeking work. Having a home recording studio enables voice actors to audition online for jobs they would otherwise never have an opportunity to try out for. I'll discuss this further in the next chapter.

So, once you've established yourself in your local market (or before if you have the cash to invest in equipment), and started making some money, a great next step is to expand your market by creating for yourself the ability to record in your own studio. Once you've done that, the possibilities are literally endless.

Making the decision to commit to creating a home recording studio was a critical first step - and probably the easiest step as it turns out. If you're not computer savvy (like yours truly), it's important to reach out to experienced professionals to help you in selecting the proper equipment for your studio. It's true that you don't need a lot of gadgets to record your voice, but getting the right gadgets for what you want to do will make all the difference in the world.

I worked with a company that specializes in providing equipment to studio professionals. They had a home recording package that provided everything I needed to get started. It wasn't inexpensive, but it also wasn't unreasonable. After all, this is a business you're starting and most businesses have start up costs, right?

I can tell you that it's very important to make sure you select a computer that is compatible with the recording software you're using. I purchased a PC, only to find out that the software (Avid Pro Tools) is much more compatible with a Mac. I ended up purchasing a refurbished Mac Book Pro and the software runs perfectly.

The essential equipment you will need to get started is:

1. A computer (make sure it's compatible with your software)

2. Recording software (I use Avid ProTools)

3. An external hard drive (Voice recordings can take up a lot of space)

4. A microphone (I use a Bluebird)

5. A device to connect your microphone to your computer (I use an M-Box mini)

You can purchase all of the necessary equipment separately online. Ebay.com or the craigslist.org site for your area are two places to check out. I have a producer friend who did this. He had his engineer check all the specs and make sure everything was compatible and he was able to save quite a bit of money by buying the equipment individually.

If you're like me though, using a company that specializes in recording equipment will eliminate all the worry of making sure the various components work together properly. They've figured all that out for you ahead of time. All you have to do is take the equipment out of the boxes and plug them in, download the software, and you're ready to start recording!

Contact me at my website mikelenzvoice.com for more information on the company I used.

Now let's discuss the physical layout of my studio and how I was able to create a space for very little money - which is good because the bulk of your money should be invested in the hardware and recording software.

First, it's important to find a space that is quiet - or as quiet as you can find in your home. This could be as simple as a closet in your bedroom. The main thing is to find and area that has minimum sound. Windows are a definite no-no. In my home, we have four children ranging in age from 14 to 2, so you can imagine my challenge in finding that special quiet place!

I chose a small area in my basement to build my humble studio. The space is at the bottom of the stairs and measures about 6 feet by 15 feet. There are no windows, and it was enclosed on three sides by sheet rock walls. I framed out the fourth wall and put a door in, thereby enclosing the space and making it a room.

The ceiling in our basement is low, which is a good thing for a recording studio. The less room there is to have sound bounce around the better. The ceiling was not sheet rocked which was another good thing because it allowed me to properly insulate for sound.

` When shopping for insulation, I came upon a type that was not fiberglass and was actually considered soundproofing insulation. This was a great find because I didn't have to worry about inhaling fiberglass during installation and could literally use my bare hands to rip the insulation and shove into all the small spaces.

After loading up the ceiling and the newly framed wall with insulation, I made another cost saving and labor saving decision. Instead of sheet rocking the ceiling (holding up heavy sheet rock over my head didn't appeal to me one bit), I bought drop ceiling panels - that's right, just the panels - and screwed them right into the joists of the ceiling. This provided another layer of sound absorbing material and saved on headroom (remember, my ceiling was low to begin with).

The last step was to throw down an area rug on the cement floor and, presto - my home studio was complete. A nicely sound minimizing room that is small and extremely functional. Don't get me wrong, I still have to tell the kids to be quiet when I'm recording, but the space is about as soundproof as I could have ever hoped for when I started out.

> ***Words of Wisdom:*** *Always be thinking ahead. Remember that your voice over career is a journey. A journey involves moving from one place to another, and your voice over career will constantly evolve over time. It's important to look ahead and make sure that you prepare yourself for the possibilities.*

When I built my home recording studio, I did so with the anticipation that it would provide me the opportunity in the future to get more voice over work. Once I had accumulated some money from my various voice-over jobs, I had to decide where to invest those funds to help grow my business (remember – this is a business!) At first I didn't get any additional work, but as I told you earlier in the book, my journey into the world of audio book narration would not have been possible had I not had a home studio to record auditions and ultimately to record the audio books that I was chosen to narrate.

Making the decision whether to build a home recording studio will be different for each voice actor. When you do get to that point, just make sure to do your homework and research. You'll be surprised how cost effectively you can create a space that will allow you to create great sounding voice-overs.

Chapter 10:

The Future

As I've said several times in this book, your voice acting career is a journey. I've given you some accounts of my own journey in hopes of helping you in yours. The big question is, what does the future hold for the voice acting industry as a whole and for all of us voice actors in particular?

It probably won't come as a surprise to hear me say that I believe the present and the future of the voice-over industry is the Internet.

In the old days (like 5 years ago) most voice-over jobs were handled in a studio by a bricks and mortar production company. In many of the large metropolitan cities, casting agents called all the shots. Oh, and if you weren't represented by a talent agency and a member of an actors union, you were pretty much out of luck.

Today, everything is wide open. Being a member of an actors union can in some ways, be detrimental to your career in voice-overs. Many producers are bypassing casting agencies and production companies all together and reaching out to voice talent directly through online companies.

What does this mean to you and your career?

Well, to begin with, you need to be more business savvy. The competition is fierce, because anyone with a computer and a microphone can call themselves a voice actor. You have to constantly work on distinguishing yourself from all the competition.

Since producers are reaching out directly to voice over talent via the internet, the expectation in many cases is that you will be able to deliver a fully produced and finished product. This is especially true in the audio book narration field. Through online sites, voice actors can submit auditions and be selected to narrate audio books.

My audio book narrating experience has taught me that you have to be prepared. It's not as simple as just reading a book out loud. My first audio book was 300 pages long and I was responsible for fully producing the book so that it was delivered to the publisher ready for sale.

This involved the preparation – reading the entire book and marking up the copy so my read would sound natural. It also involved all of the editing, which is a critical part of the process.

Since editing is not my strong point, I partnered with a fellow voice actor who was also an audio engineer. Remember, I was responsible for the final product, so I either had to do it all myself or find someone who could help; there was no production studio to fall back on, it was all on me!

We recorded over 15 hours of audio and my editor spent at least 45 hours editing. The next step was to listen back to the entire book while following along the manuscript to check for any errors. Once that was completed, we had to re-record any edits that we had found and finally master all the files and upload them to the publisher.

If it sounds like a lot of work – it was. In the old days, a voice actor would walk into a production studio and read the book. The production studio would handle all of the editing and mastering.

Those days are over.

I've never met the publishers of the audio books I've narrated. All of our communication has been via email and an occasional phone call. More and more of the work I do is handled through the Internet, and our production company that started out as two friends having breakfast, has developed into one that provides not only audiobook narration, but also audio and video services to our clients – the bulk of which is handled online.

> ***Words of Wisdom:*** *Learn all you can about the voice over industry and stay on top of all of the latest*

*developments. This industry is
changing rapidly. It's more
important than ever to understand
basic computer programs that allow
you to record and edit your work. Pro
Tools is the industry standard when it
comes to recording software, but
there are other, less expensive
options out there, like Audacity, so do
your research and learn. Also, make
sure that you network with other
studio professionals who can help
you on your projects. If technology is
your thing, then dive in and become
an expert. If it's not, then make sure
you have the resources around you to
deliver professional projects every
time.*

I believe the future of voice acting is
exciting, and filled with possibilities. There
is no question that this is the best time to
get involved in this incredible industry. I
hope your journey is filled with much
success, and if this book helps guide you a
bit along your path, I'm grateful to have had
the opportunity to help you in some small
way.

If you have any questions please don't hesitate to send me a message at my website mikelenzvoice.com.

In the meantime - Keep Talking!

Made in the USA
San Bernardino, CA
22 December 2019

62256944R00038